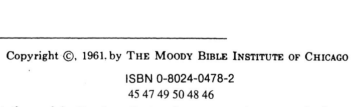

Copyright ©, 1961, by THE MOODY BIBLE INSTITUTE OF CHICAGO

ISBN 0-8024-0478-2

45 47 49 50 48 46

The Author used the King James Version when preparing the questions for this manual.

Printed in the United States of America

Basic Bible Study For New Christians

(Formerly *Basic Bible Work for Young Believers*)

This is a self-study course designed to help you discover for yourself, from the Bible, some important basic truths concerning salvation and the Christian life.

how to study the lesson

1. Try to find a quiet spot free from distractions and noise.

2. Read each question carefully.

3. Look up the Scripture reference given after each question. Make sure you have found the correct Scripture passage. For example, sometimes you will find yourself looking up JOHN 1:1 instead of I JOHN 1:1.

4. Answer the question from the appropriate Bible passage. Write, in your own words, a phrase or sentence to answer the question. In questions that can be answered with a "yes" or "no" always give the reason for your answer . . . "Yes, because. . . ."

5. If possible, keep a dictionary handy in order to look up words you don't understand.

6. Pray for God's help. You *need* God's help in order to understand what you study in the Bible. Psalm 119:18 would be an appropriate verse for you to take to God in prayer.

7. *Class teachers using this course for group study will find some helpful suggestions on page 47.*

how to take the self-check tests

Each lesson is concluded with a test designed to help you evaluate what you have learned.

1. Review the lesson carefully in the light of the self-check test questions.

2. If there are any questions in the self-check test you cannot answer, perhaps you have written into your lesson the wrong answer from your Bible. Go over your work carefully to make sure you have filled in the blanks correctly.

3. When you think you are ready to take the self-check test, do so without looking up the answers.

4. Check your answers to the self-check test carefully with the answer key given on page 48.

5. If you have any questions wrong, your answer key will tell you where to find the correct answer in your lesson. Go back and locate the right answers. Learn by your mistakes!

apply what you have learned to your own life

In this connection, read carefully JAMES 1:22-25. It is only as you apply your lessons to your own life that you will really grow in grace and increase in the knowledge of God.

Some Truths About the Bible

1. Where is the best place to keep your Bible?

PSALM 119:11 _____ _____

Difficult portions in the Bible

2. Will you always understand easily all you read in the Bible?

II PETER 3:15, 16 _____

3. Did the disciples always understand the words of Jesus?

LUKE 9:43-45 _____

4. What promise did Jesus give them?

JOHN 16:12, 13 _____

_____

5. What would be a good prayer for us to offer before beginning Bible study?

PSALM 119:18 _____

_____

How to test all religious teachings

6. What is the best way to judge all religious teachings?

ISAIAH 8:20 _____

_____

"It isn't the Bible but the expounders of the Bible that cause diversities of teaching in Christendom. The fault rests with the fallen, corrupt nature of man, which so affects him that he fails clearly to discern truth, even when it is set before his eyes. Do not go to your Bible with stereotype ideas which you seek to confirm, but with an open mind, seeking to discover what God says. The tracks of some popular teachings, traced back through Church history, will lead you to the very entrance of the enemy's camp."

The message of the Bible

7. Who is spoken of throughout the Bible?

LUKE 24:27 _____

8. What is the very heart of the Bible message concerning this One?

I PETER 2:24 _____

_____

_____

9. The following verses mention three purposes for which the Bible was given to us:

a. JOHN 20:31 _____

_____

b. ROMANS 15:4 _____

_____

c. I CORINTHIANS 10:11 _____

_____

What to do with your Bible

(1) Study it through—JOSHUA 1:8
(2) Pray it in—PSALM 119:18
(3) Write it down—ISAIAH 30:8
(4) Work it out—JAMES 1:22
(5) Pass it on—PSALM 119:27, 46

The important question is, not how many times you have been through the Bible, but how many times the Bible has been through you.

The Bible is God's eternal Word

10. What claim is made for the Bible?

II TIMOTHY 3:16, 17 _____

_____

11. By what process did God reveal His thoughts to humanity?

II PETER 1:21_____

_____

12. In what way can you account for the superiority of the Bible over human philosophy?

I CORINTHIANS 2:13_____

_____

Writers of Scripture affirm that their words are divinely taught. This, of course, refers to original documents, not to translations and versions; but the labors of competent scholars have brought our English versions to such a degree of accuracy that we may confidently rest upon them as authoritative in all essential points.

I CORINTHIANS 2:9-14 gives the process by which truth passed from the mind of God to the minds of His servants: (a) Unseen things of God are undiscoverable by the natural man (v. 9). (b) These things God has revealed to chosen men (vv. 10-12). (c) These things are communicated in Spirit-taught words (v. 13). This does not imply mechanical dictation or the effacement of the writer's personality, but only that the Spirit guided in the choice of words from the writer's own vocabulary (v. 13). These Spirit-taught words of the Bible are spiritually discerned only by those having the Holy Spirit in them (I CORINTHIANS 2:15, 16).

13. What did Jesus say as to His words?

MATTHEW 24:35 _____

_____

14. Is it permissible to add to or subtract from the Word of God?

DEUTERONOMY 4:2_____

Progress in your spiritual life

15. List some important conditions of spiritual progress.

PSALM 1:2 _____

a. _____

b. _____

16. What is the best way to find guidance upon your daily path?

PSALM 119:105 _____

_____

17. What is God's Word able to do for you?

ACTS 20:32 _____

_____

18. What did Jesus do to defeat Satan in the hour of temptation?

MATTHEW 4:4, 7, 10 _____

_____

6

check-up time No. 1

You have just studied some important truths about the Bible. Review your study by rereading the questions and your written answers. If you wish, you may use the self-check test as an aid in reviewing your lesson. If you aren't sure of an answer, reread the Scripture portion given to see if you can find the answer. Then take this test to see how well you understand important truths you have studied.

In the right-hand margin write "True" or "False" after each of the following statements.

1. There are no difficult portions in the Bible. _____

2. The best way to judge all religious teachings is to compare them with the Scriptures. _____

3. The Bible was given by God through men who were moved by the Holy Spirit. _____

4. The disciples always understood the words of Jesus. _____

5. God uses the Bible as a means of guiding His children. _____

6. The Holy Spirit leads believers into all truth. _____

7. Tradition carries as much weight for spiritual instruction as the Bible does. _____

8. The fruitful believer is one who daily meditates on God's Word. _____

9. The Lord Jesus defeated temptation by arguing with Satan. _____

10. It is well to offer a prayer for enlightenment before studying God's Word. _____

Turn to page 48 and check your answers.

God's
Way of Salvation

What the Bible reveals

1. What is the great purpose of the revelation of Scripture?

JOHN 20:31 _____

Man's blindness to the gospel

2. Why can't some people understand the Bible?

I CORINTHIANS 2:14; 1:18_____

_____

3. What is the explanation of the fact that many educated men of the world do not accept the Bible message concerning salvation?

ISAIAH 55:8, 9_____

_____

The Bible exposes man's sin

4. Why do sinful men dislike the Bible?

JOHN 3:19, 20 _____

5. How does the Bible search men's hearts?

HEBREWS 4:12 _____

8

God's Word will prevail

6. What is the best way to find out whether or not the Bible is God's Word?

a. HEBREWS 10:16_____

_____

b. JOHN 7:17_____

_____

c. I JOHN 5:10 _____

_____

The Holy Spirit bears witness to the truth of the Bible, and the vital experience given to those who accept Christ is the final answer to all assaults upon the Word of God. Christianity still works powerfully wherever it is truly accepted.

7. What is said about the gospel of Christ?

ROMANS 1:16_____

Ideas about salvation

8. Will a way of salvation which a person has devised for himself, even though there is much good about it, suffice to bring the soul to God?

a. ISAIAH 53:6 _____

_____

b. ISAIAH 55:8 _____

_____

c. JOHN 14:6 _____

_____

9. Is it possible that a way that seems right to a person may be altogether the wrong way to be saved?

PROVERBS 14:12 _____

_____

Is salvation by works?

10. What does the Bible say about salvation by personal merit?

a. GALATIANS 2:16 _____

_____

b. EPHESIANS 2:8, 9 _____

_____

c. ROMANS 4:5 _____

_____

d. TITUS 3:5, 6 _____

_____

e. II TIMOTHY 1:9 _____

_____

11. Is there such a thing as personal righteousness of sufficient value to purchase eternal life?

ISAIAH 64:6 _____

_____

What must man acknowledge?

12. What must a person acknowledge before he can be saved?

a. ROMANS 3:23 _____

b. LUKE 15:18 _____

c. LUKE 18:13 _____

13. Will God listen to those who are truly repentant?

ISAIAH 55:7 _____

The cost of man's redemption

14. What is God's remedy for sin?

I CORINTHIANS 15:3-5 _____

_____

_____

15. What price did sin call for before men could be saved?

I PETER 1:18, 19 _____

_____

_____

16. On what terms does God make salvation available to the sinner?

ROMANS 6:23_____

Believing and receiving Christ

17. What is the only way of salvation?

a. JOHN 3:16_____

_____

b. JOHN 1:12_____

_____

18. Why are people lost?

a. JOHN 3:36 _____

_____

b. JOHN 16:9 _____

_____

19. How can the unbeliever pass from spiritual death into eternal life?

JOHN 5:24 _____

_____

Christ died for sinners

20. Are there any who are such great sinners that God cannot save them?

ISAIAH 1:18 _____

_____

21. For what class of people did Christ make His sacrifice?

LUKE 19:10 _____

22. How many does this include?

ISAIAH 53:6 _____

23. What did Paul say?

I TIMOTHY 1:15 _____

_____

_____

When can a person be saved?

24. When is the best time to consider the question of one's eternal destiny?

a. II CORINTHIANS 6:2 _____

_____

b. ISAIAH 55:6 _____

_____

c. HEBREWS 3:13 _____

_____

25. Why is it important to give heed immediately to the drawing power of the Holy Spirit?

JOHN 6:44 _____

Does it last?

26. When Christ saves from the penalty of sin, can He also keep the believer from the power of sin?

a. JUDE 24 _____

b. I PETER 1:5 _____

c. PHILIPPIANS 1:6 _____

_____

27. Why does Christ's power to save extend throughout life—and forever?

HEBREWS 7:25 _____

_____

You have just studied some important truths about salvation. Review your study by rereading the questions and your written answers. If you aren't sure of an answer, reread the Scripture portion given to see if you can find the answer. Then take the following test to see how well you understand important truths you have studied.

check-up time No. 2

In the right-hand margin write "True" or "False" after each of the following statements.

1. The Bible can be understood by everybody. _____

2. Sinful men often dislike the Bible because it searches their hearts. _____

3. Salvation must be accepted as a free gift from God. _____

4. It doesn't matter what a person believes as long as he is sincere. _____

5. It is a good thing to postpone considering the question of salvation until later in life, when one's opinions will be more mature. _____

6. The gospel is declared to be the power of God unto salvation to everyone who believes it. _____

7. The Bible encourages people to do the best they can in order to have God's approval. _____

8. The Lord Jesus paid the penalty of sin. _____

9. There are some people who are too bad to be saved. _____

10. Paul told Timothy that Christ died for sinners and that he (Paul) was the chief of them. _____

Turn to page 48 and check your answers.

Our Blessings in Christ

The moment we truly accept Christ we are justified by faith. (The word "justified" means that we are "made as though we had never sinned in the sight of God.") God has much more for us than this, however. Let us see what it really means to possess all that God holds out to the Christian.

Heirs of life eternal

1. If one is truly a member of Christ's flock, what promise has he?

JOHN 10:28 _____

2. What will be the climax of this life in Christ?

II TIMOTHY 1:9, 10 _____

3. What does God say to those who will come apart from the world that rejects Christ, and live the separated life?

II CORINTHIANS 6:17, 18 _____

Joint heirs with Christ

4. If we are God's children, what more can be said of us?

ROMANS 8:17_____

5. If the Holy Spirit is in our hearts, what follows?

GALATIANS 4:6, 7 _____

_____

Complete salvation

6. Who intercedes for the believer, even though, in a moment of weakness, he commits a sin?

I JOHN 2:1, 2 _____

_____

_____

7. Is our salvation dependent on our own efforts to live good lives?

HEBREWS 7:25 _____

_____

God chastens His children

8. How does God deal with His children who backslide and become disobedient?

HEBREWS 12:5-9_____

_____

9. Why are Christians thus dealt with?

I CORINTHIANS 11:31, 32 _____

_____

10. Even though one who is truly on the foundation, Jesus Christ, may lose reward by not serving Him as he should, what is his eternal destiny?

I CORINTHIANS 3:11, 15 _____

_____

11. Can one live a happy Christian life even while he is disobedient?

PSALM 32:2-5 _____

_____

If we sin ...

12. What should we do when we realize that we have sinned?

ISAIAH 55:7 _____

_____

13. What will God do then?

I JOHN 1:9 _____

_____

Test salvation for reality

14. What should justification give us?

ROMANS 5:1 _____

_____

15. On what basis alone do we know that we are God's children?

GALATIANS 3:26 _____

_____

16. What is one of the earliest proofs that we are truly saved?

I JOHN 3:14 _____

_____

The crowning day is coming

17. Over and above the salvation we have in Christ, what shall we receive at the judgment seat of Christ?

I Corinthians 3:14; II Corinthians 5:10 _____

_____

18. If we want to receive great reward, what must we do?

Luke 6:35 _____

_____

19. What does Paul exhort us to do?

I Corinthians 9:24 _____

_____

Guidance for every day

20. What promise is given us for all our daily perplexities and duties?

Isaiah 58:11 _____

_____

21. If we want to follow God's teaching, who will show us the way to go?

Isaiah 48:17 _____

_____

22. What is a sure way of securing divine direction?

Proverbs 3:6 _____

_____

God guards His children

23. What assurance may a Christian have at all times?

Romans 8:38, 39 _____

_____

24. By what power will he be kept to the end?

I PETER 1:5_____

_____

God makes full provision

25. Need we worry about material needs?

PHILIPPIANS 4:19 _____

_____

26. Need we worry about our ability to carry on?

PHILIPPIANS 4:13 _____

_____

When a Christian dies

27. Even if we face death, what is our comfort?

PHILIPPIANS 1:21 _____

_____

28. What always awaits us ahead?

I PETER 1:4_____

_____

_____

check-up time No. 3

_____

What have you learned in this lesson? Review the lesson in the light of the self-check test below. Check carefully any questions you can't answer. Be sure you have filled in the blanks correctly. When you think you are ready, take the test without looking up the answers.

In the right-hand margin write "True" or "False" after each of the following statements.

1. An early proof of true salvation is to be found in real love for fellow Christians. _____

2. Those who are truly saved are made joint heirs with Christ. _____

3. When a believer dies, he goes immediately to be with Christ. _____

4. The Christian has an Advocate to plead his cause before God. _____

5. The Christian should learn to overlook his sins because he has eternal life. _____

6. Many things can happen which can separate a Christian from the love of Christ. _____

7. God wants to help us make right and wise decisions. _____

8. God will tolerate sin in His children. _____

9. Justification gives us peace with God. _____

10. A Christian who is disobedient to God can know true happiness at the same time. _____

Turn to page 48 and check your answers.

The Consecrated Life

To grow in grace is the first duty and privilege of the believer in the Lord Jesus Christ. Those who stop growing intellectually soon die intellectually. The same holds true in the spiritual life. Growth is the proof of life. Our Saviour desires that we mount up into "heavenly places."

When a man is going up in a balloon, he takes bags of sand as ballast; and when he wants to mount higher, he throws some of the sand out. The more he throws out, the higher he goes. If we want to mount to the heights of spiritual blessing, we must throw overboard the things of the flesh, the world and the devil. The measure of our happiness in life will be in proportion to our surrender to Christ.

The believer's body

1. What is the reasonable and spiritual service for a Christian to render?

ROMANS 12:1

2. What two facts should every Christian know?

I CORINTHIANS 6:19

3. In view of the indwelling of the Holy Spirit and divine ownership, what should be our aim?

I CORINTHIANS 6:20

The believer's mind

4. What do we discover for ourselves if we turn from worldly things to the Christ-life?

ROMANS 12:2_____

_____

The secret of victory over sin

5. If Christ Himself possesses us, by what power are we motivated?

GALATIANS 2:20 _____

_____

6. What is the chief essential of a fruitful Christian life?

JOHN 15:4, 5 _____

_____

To abide in Christ is to allow no known sin to go unjudged and unconfessed; to have no interest into which Christ is not brought; no life which He cannot share. It means that we take all burdens to Him and draw our wisdom and strength from Him. Nothing is allowed which separates from Him.

The Christian's goal

7. What should be the one goal before us?

PHILIPPIANS 3:13, 14_____

_____

8. If we are risen to a new life in Christ, what will be our *innermost* desire?

COLOSSIANS 3:1, 2 _____

_____

9. Unto whom will our eyes be turned?

HEBREWS 12:2 _____

_____

10. If our eyes are really on Him, what will follow?

HEBREWS 12:1 _____

_____

11. What should be our *constant* desire?

COLOSSIANS 3:17 _____

_____

God's standards for His children

12. What should we seek to add to our faith in Christ?

II PETER 1:5-8 _____

_____

13. Having such promises in Christ, what should our desire naturally be?

II CORINTHIANS 7:1 _____

_____

The warfare of the Christian

14. What should be our daily resolution?

GALATIANS 5:1 _____

_____

15. To live a victorious life, what do we need?

EPHESIANS 6:11 _____

_____

16. What are the parts of our Christian armor?
EPHESIANS 6:13-17

a. _____   d. _____

b. _____   e. _____

c. _____   f. _____

The importance of a daily Quiet Time

17. In order to live such a life, what must be our daily practice?

ISAIAH 40:31 _____

_____

18. In what way should Bible *study* have a practical relationship to our daily lives?

JAMES 1:22-24_____

_____

The Christian's testimony

19. Need we be concerned as to how worldly people regard our Christian stand?

MATTHEW 5:16_____

_____

20. How must we meet the inconsistencies of those about us?

I PETER 2:15_____

_____

Going all the way

21. To what limit should a true Christian be willing to go, in view of all Christ has done for him?

MARK 8:34, 35 _____

_____

check-up time No. 4

You have just studied some important truths about the consecrated life. Review your study by rereading the questions and your written answers. If you aren't sure of an answer, reread the Scripture portion given to see if you can find the answer. Then take this test to see how well you understand important truths you have studied.

In the right-hand margin write "True" or "False" after each of the following statements.

1. The believer's body may be considered to be his own property.　_____

2. The Bible is described as the Sword of the Spirit.　_____

3. Christ tells the believer to abide in Him.　_____

4. Christ abides in the Christian.　_____

5. The believer is to run the Christian race patiently.　_____

6. There are some things in the Christian life which cannot be done in Christ's name.　_____

7. The Christian is to take a firm stand against being brought into bondage.　_____

8. The Author and Finisher of our faith is Jesus.　_____

9. True believers should be willing to surrender to Christ, even unto death.　_____

10. The Christian should sincerely desire to be holy.　_____

Turn to page 48 and check your answers.

How to Meet Temptation

It is a grievous error to think that we escape temptation by becoming Christians. We may escape the baser forms of temptation, but there are subtle snares which Satan lays for the believers' feet constantly.

Everybody is tempted

1. What exhortation is given the Christian?

I CORINTHIANS 10:12 _____

2. Can any child of God safely say he has attained sinless perfection?

I JOHN 1:8, 10 _____

Why God allows us to be tempted

The fact that a Christian cannot altogether escape temptation shows that God has some purpose in it. Let us see if we can discover what that purpose is.

3. What may be accomplished in us by the trying of our faith?

JAMES 1:2-4 _____

4. What limit does God set upon temptation which He permits to come to us?

I CORINTHIANS 10:13_____

_____

_____

5. What promise is given us which can make us ever victorious?

I CORINTHIANS 10:13_____

_____

6. Will God especially reward those who let Him give victory in time of temptation?

JAMES 1:12 _____

_____

The source of temptation

7. Does God ever tempt us?

JAMES 1:13 _____

8. What does the Lord do for His own who are about to be subjected to temptation?

LUKE 22:31, 32_____

_____

9. How do the following verses show one source of temptation?

a. JAMES 1:14 _____

_____

b. MARK 7:21-23 _____

_____

10. What is the Holy Spirit always saying to the child of God?

I Peter 2:11 _____

_____

11. From what outer source do evil suggestions come?

Matthew 4:1, 8, 9; I Corinthians 7:5; II Corinthians 4:4;

Ephesians 6:12 _____

_____

12. Why must we always be vigilant?

I Peter 5:8; II Corinthians 2:11 _____

_____

13. What must always be our attitude toward worldly ways?

I John 2:15-17 _____

_____

_____

14. Is it possible to be both worldly and spiritual at the same time?
James 4:4 _____

_____

How to overcome temptation

15. In some kinds of temptation, what is the proper course to take?
James 4:7 _____

_____

16. In other cases, what should be done?

I TIMOTHY 6:10, 11; II TIMOTHY 2:22 _____

_____

17. If there is any doubt as to what to do, what is always the safe course?

MATTHEW 26:41 _____

18. What are two great sources of power for overcoming temptation?

REVELATION 12:11 _____

_____

19. What care must a Christian take, even in trying to save others from temptation?

GALATIANS 6:1 _____

_____

20. Should a Christian take unnecessary chances?

I CORINTHIANS 5:11 _____

21. What is the sure way to keep on the right path?

PSALM 119:9 _____

22. What experience of the Lord Jesus gives great comfort to the tempted Christian?

HEBREWS 2:18; 4:15, 16 _____

_____

_____

check-up time No. 5

You have just studied some important truths about temptation. Review your study by rereading the questions and your written answers. If you aren't sure of an answer, reread the Scripture portion given to see if you can find the answer. Then take this test to see how well you understand important truths you have studied.

In the right-hand margin write "True" or "False" after each of the following statements.

1. Sinless perfection can be attained in this life. _____

2. All temptations come *directly* from Satan. _____

3. God has a purpose in allowing Christians to be tempted. _____

4. With every temptation that comes to the believer in Christ, God provides a way of escape. _____

5. Even the Lord Jesus was tempted. _____

6. It is possible to be worldly and spiritual at the same time. _____

7. God rewards His children who overcome in the hour of temptation. _____

8. The Christian should flee from Satan. _____

9. When the believer is tempted, it is important for him to remember that God knows about it and can deliver from it. _____

10. There are some things from which, as Christians, we are to abstain. _____

Turn to page 48 and check your answers.

How to Pray

Except for the necessity of obtaining spiritual food from the Word of God, nothing is so important to the Christian as to learn how to pray.

We must pray because there is a devil who seeks the downfall of God's children (EPHESIANS 6:12, 13); because prayer is the appointed way to receive blessings (JAMES 4:2); because our Lord Himself prayed (MARK 1:35); because prayer leads to fullness of joy (JOHN 16:24).

In the childhood of our faith, we may make poor use of the weapons of prayer; but when we come to maturity as Christians, we may learn to obtain the things for which we ask (I JOHN 5:14).

The basis and motive for prayer

1. On what basis are we to approach God in prayer?

JOHN 16:23 _____

2. As we come to God on the merits of His Son, what motive should prompt our asking?

JOHN 14:13, 14 _____

_____

Important conditions for effectual prayer

3. What is one of the first conditions for effective prayer?

I PETER 3:12; I TIMOTHY 2:8 _____

4. In view of this condition to answered prayer, what should be our daily petition?

PSALM 139:23, 24 _____

_____

_____

5. What is another condition for effective prayer?

MATTHEW 21:22; MARK 11:24; JAMES 1:6, 7 _____

_____

It is impossible for the Christian to exercise real faith that God will grant something which is contrary to His expressed will in the Bible, or that He will grant something which the believer has reason to think would not be for His glory. The Holy Spirit, after all, gives us the confidence we need in asking; and we must be sure that we desire His leading in our prayers (ROMANS 8:26; JUDE 20; EPHESIANS 6:18).

6. What two conditions for effectual prayer did the Lord Jesus lay down?

JOHN 15:7 _____

_____

7. What did John give as essentials for effective prayer?

I JOHN 3:22_____

_____

_____

8. Should a person expect answers to prayer while harboring a bitter spirit in his heart?

MARK 11:25 _____

The right attitude in prayer

9. How should we approach God?

a. ECCLESIASTES 5:2 _____

b. JOHN 9:31 _____

32

10. How should we draw near to God?

HEBREWS 10:22 _____ _____ _____

11. What attitude will incline God toward a person?

PSALM 34:18 _____ _____ _____

12. What spirit should accompany all our asking?

EPHESIANS 5:20; I THESSALONIANS 5:18; PHILIPPIANS 4:6___

United prayer

13. Should we do more than pray by ourselves?

MATTHEW 18:19 _____ _____ _____

Why some prayers are unanswered

14. Why are some prayers not answered?

JEREMIAH 29:13 _ _____ _____ ____

15. What often robs prayer of its power?

a. JAMES 4:3 _____

b. PSALM 66:18 _____

c. EZEKIEL 14:3 _____

d. PROVERBS 21:13 _____

16. What is especially displeasing to God?

MATTHEW 6:7, 8_____

33

When to pray

17. When should we pray?

a. PSALM 5:3 _____

b. PSALM 55:17 _____

c. MATTHEW 26:41 _____

d. LUKE 21:36; EPHESIANS 6:18 _____

e. I THESSALONIANS 5:17 _____

f. HEBREWS 4:16 _____

Petitions to ask

18. For what especially should we pray?

a. I TIMOTHY 2:2 _____

b. II THESSALONIANS 3:1, 2 _____

c. I TIMOTHY 2:1 _____

d. MATTHEW 5:44 _____

e. PHILIPPIANS 4:6 _____

f. PSALM 51:1-4 _____

g. JAMES 1:5 _____

h. PSALM 19:12 _____

i. REVELATION 22:20 _____

check-up time No. 6

You have just studied some important truths about prayer. Review your study by rereading the questions and your written answers. If you aren't sure of an answer, reread the Scripture portion given to see if you can find the answer. Then take this test to see how well you understand important truths you have studied.

In the right-hand margin write "True" or "False" after each of the following statements.

1. Prayer should be offered in the name of the Lord Jesus. _____

2. It is a good practice to repeat the same words constantly in prayer. _____

3. Prayer should be offered only at regular intervals. _____

4. Unconfessed sin can hinder the answer to our prayers. _____

5. Public prayer is too formal to be effective. _____

6. Thanksgiving and prayer should be kept separate. _____

7. An unforgiving spirit hinders prayer. _____

8. It is important to believe that God will answer when we pray. _____

9. It is too much to expect the Christian to pray for his enemies. _____

10. Sometimes we ask for the wrong things when we pray. _____

Turn to page 48 and check your answers.

Building a Christian Character

One cannot enter into Bible study without discovering immediately that development of Christian character is expected of him, and that the power of the Holy Spirit is pledged to the believer who surrenders to Him. By His power alone can the Christian grow in grace and in the knowledge of the Lord (II PETER 3:18).

Some of our responsibilities

1. What is said of those who claim to be Christians but give no heed to the ethical teachings of Christ?

I TIMOTHY 6:3, 4 _____

_____

_____

2. Who is counted great among those who serve Christ?

MATTHEW 5:19 _____

_____

3. According to the words of the Lord Jesus, how do we prove to the world the reality of our conversion?

JOHN 13:34, 35 _____

4. Is it impossible to practice the ethical commands of Christ?

I JOHN 5:2, 3 _____

5. Why do His commands always carry with them the ability we need to obey them?

JOHN 15:5 _____

_____

The following are some of the Christian qualities which we have already noted in our study as being essential to a well-rounded life. Every Christian may possess them by the help of the Holy Spirit.

Stability in the Christian life

6. What is Paul's exhortation?

I CORINTHIANS 15:58 _____

_____

7. What qualities obviously should be seen in the life of a Christian?

I THESSALONIANS 5:8 _____

_____

8. What firm resolution should every Christian make?

HEBREWS 4:14 _____

"The royal law"

JAMES 2:8

9. What quality should always be displayed?

ROMANS 13:10 _____

10. To whom should this spirit of love extend?

MATTHEW 5:44; ROMANS 13:8 _____

_____

To see how love works, read I CORINTHIANS 13.

The golden rule

11. By what rule do we decide what our conduct should be in dealing with others?

MATTHEW 7:12 _____

_____

Overcoming evil with good

12. What rule is to guide us when evil is done to us?

ROMANS 12:21 _____

13. What spirit should always be manifest toward those who injure us?

COLOSSIANS 3:13 _____

Humility

14. What did Jesus name as one of the first Christian graces?

MATTHEW 5:3 _____

15. What is Paul's exhortation?

ROMANS 12:16 _____

_____

_____

16. To whom does God give special promise of grace?

I PETER 5:5 _____

Purity

17. What quality must a Christian have if he is to "see God"?

MATTHEW 5:8 _____

18. What should we always strive to maintain?

I PETER 3:16_____

19. What is the great reason why we should strive for holiness?
I PETER 1:15_____

20. Why did Christ give Himself for us?

TITUS 2:14_____

_____

_____

21. Since we are bought with such a price, what should we do?

I CORINTHIANS 6:20_____

_____

22. Can the purifying process go on apart from faith in Christ?
ACTS 15:9 _____

God cannot use us if we are indifferent to the claims of purity, careless about being "unspotted from the world" (JAMES 1:27). God is always merciful to those who have fallen and become spotted through weakness or a sudden temptation; but nothing can compensate for a thoughtless and careless life in which the soul shows no concern about keeping pure.

Peace within and without

23. Who can impart peace to our hearts?

JOHN 14:27 _____

24. Under all circumstances, what should rule our hearts?

COLOSSIANS 3:15 _____

25. What should we follow after?

HEBREWS 12:14 _____

_____

Rendering "unto God the things that are God's"

26. According to II CORINTHIANS 9:7, whom does God love?

_____

27. What promise is given in PROVERBS 11:25?

_____

_____

28. Is it the amount of money in the gift that counts with God?
II CORINTHIANS 8:12; MARK 12:43, 44 _____

_____

29. Is God any man's debtor?

MALACHI 3:8-10 _____ _____

In I CORINTHIANS 16:2 Paul sets forth a threefold rule for giving: (1) "upon the first day of the week"; (2) "lay by . . . in store"; (3) "as God hath prospered."

Personal integrity and graciousness

30. What quality is always to be cultivated?

ROMANS 12:17; II CORINTHIANS 8:21; ROMANS 13:13 _____

_____

31. What about our speech?

EPHESIANS 4:25 _____

32. What about the disposition?

a. PROVERBS 16:24 _____

b. PROVERBS 15:1 _____

c. PROVERBS 19:11 _____

40

Contentment and diligence

33. What do we need to learn?

PHILIPPIANS 4:11; HEBREWS 13:5 _____

_____

34. What qualities should be displayed in all business and social relationships?

a. I THESSALONIANS 4:11 _____

b. HEBREWS 6:11, 12 _____

c. ROMANS 12:11 _____

check-up time No. 7

You have just studied some important truths about Christian character. Review your study by rereading the questions and your written answers. If you aren't sure of an answer, reread the Scripture pôrtion given to see if you can find the answer. Then take this test to see how well you understand important truths you have studied.

In the right-hand margin write "True" or "False" after each of the following statements.

1. We should forgive others even as Christ forgave us. _____

2. We should do unto others as they do unto us. _____

3. One of the first evidences of a real conversion is love for one another. _____

4. The Bible says that without Christ we can do nothing. _____

5. The Christian should always be diligent at work. _____

6. It is the amount of our gift that counts with God. _____

7. The Christian should retaliate when someone tries to quarrel with him. _____

8. God loves a cheerful giver. _____

9. A Christian should try to keep up with the Joneses. _____

10. God expects Christians to maintain clean consciences. _____

Turn to page 48 and check your answers.

Witnessing for Christ to Others

Open confession of Christ is an essential accompaniment of salvation (ROMANS 10:9, 10). Saving faith is bound to express itself, not only through the life, but also through the lips, for "out of the abundance of the heart the mouth speaketh" (MATTHEW 12:34). This is one of the great means of growth in the Christian life. Only two other experiences are so vitally necessary—prayer and Bible study. The waters of the Dead Sea are dead because this sea is always receiving, never giving out. If we are all the while hearing gospel truths and keeping them to ourselves, we become stagnant Christians. Indeed, one's unwillingness to let others know that he is a Christian may be proof that he is not truly a Christian.

Every Christian's duty

1. What is an important truth for a Christian to learn?

PSALM 96:2; MATTHEW 5:15, 16 _____

_____

2. What is the believer obliged to declare among the people?

ISAIAH 12:4; ACTS 4:20 _____

_____

3. What is every Christian supposed to be?

ISAIAH 43:10; ACTS 1:8 _____

_____

4. When should we talk about the things of God?

DEUTERONOMY 6:7 _____

_____

5. What two things should every Christian do?

I PETER 3:15_____

_____

_____

6. Name one class of people to whom we should bear witness.
MARK 5:19 _____

Self-examination

7. Before one can effectively bear witness for Christ, what must he be and do?

PHILIPPIANS 2:15, 16_____

_____

8. In witnessing for Christ, are we to talk about our own goodness?

PSALM 71:24 _____

_____

9. Is it implied that there is to be any boasting through pride?

PSALM 34:2 _____

_____

The first duty of every Christian is to lay no stumbling block in another's way (ROMANS 14:13). God's glory is preached, not by words alone, but by conduct first of all. We cannot succeed in telling others what Christ is like unless we first show them that He can make us Christlike (JOHN 17:23).

Confessing Christ

10. If we deny Christ, what may we expect?

II TIMOTHY 2:12 _____

11. What part does confessing Christ have in genuine conversion?
ROMANS 10:9, 10 _____

_____

12. What is one way a believer has of showing that God indwells him?

I John 4:15_____

_____

13. Before whom will faithful witnesses be acknowledged?

Luke 12:8 _____

"Not ashamed" to witness

14. Should a saved person be ashamed to witness for Christ?

II Timothy 1:8, 9 _____

_____

15. Upon whom must we always rely in witnessing?

Acts 4:31 _____

16. Why was Paul not ashamed to bear witness for Christ?

Romans 1:16_____

_____

_____

17. Why did many of the rulers of the Jews not confess Christ?

John 12:42, 43 _____

_____

Faithful, even unto death

18. What helps the believer to overcome the devil?

Revelation 12:11 _____

Those who do not witness for Christ are often weak in faith, fearful of heart, without assurance of victory. Those who speak out for Christ not only fortify themselves but they also grow in grace much faster than those who keep silent.

You have just studied some important truths about witnessing. Review your study by rereading the questions and your written answers. If you aren't sure of an answer, reread the Scripture portion given to see if you can find the answer. Then take this test to see how well you understand the important truths you have studied.

In the right-hand margin write "True" or "False" after each of the following statements.

1. Paul was unashamed of the gospel. _____

2. The fear of man hinders some Christians in their witness. _____

3. Confessing Christ is one way of showing that one is truly indwelt by God. _____

4. The things of God are to be a vital part of a Christian's conversation. _____

5. A good education an extrovert personality, and a knowledge of the Bible are the full requirements of a believer for an effective witness. _____

6. A true believer is under an obligation to testify for Christ. _____

7. When a Christian leads a soul to Christ, he has much reason to boast. _____

8. We can overlook inconsistencies in our lives as long as we testify for the Lord. _____

9. Satan opposes effective Christian testimony. _____

10. All our friends should know where we stand as Christians. _____

Turn to page 48 and check your answers.

Suggestions for class use

1. The class teacher may wish to tear this page from each workbook as the answer key is on the reverse side.

2. The teacher should study the lesson first, filling in the blanks in the workbook. He should be prepared to give help to the class on some of the harder places in the lesson. He should also take the self-check tests himself, check his answers with the answer key and look up any question answered incorrectly.

3. Class sessions can be supplemented by the teacher's giving a talk or leading a discussion on the subject to be studied. The class could then fill in the workbook together as a group, in teams, or individually. If so desired by the teacher, however, this could be done at home. The self-check tests can be done as homework by the class.

4. The self-check tests can be corrected at the beginning of each class session. A brief discussion of the answers can serve as review for the previous lesson.

5. The teacher should motivate and encourage his students. Some public recognition might well be given to class members who successfully complete this course.

Moody Press, a ministry of the Moody Bible Institute, is designed for education, evangelization and edification. If we may assist you in knowing more about Christ and the Christian life, please write us without obligation to: Moody Press, c/o MLM, Chicago, Illinois 60610.

answer key
to self-check tests

Be sure to look up any questions you answered incorrectly.

Q gives the number of the test *question*.

A gives the correct *answer*.

R *refers* you back to the number of the question in the lesson itself, where the correct answer is to be found.

Mark with an "x" your wrong answers.

TEST 1			TEST 2			TEST 3			TEST 4		
Q	A	R	Q	A	R	Q	A	R	Q	A	R
1	F	2	1	F	2	1	T	16	1	F	2
2	T	6	2	T	4	2	T	4	2	T	16
3	T	11	3	T	16	3	T	27	3	T	6
4	F	3	4	F	9	4	T	6	4	T	6
5	T	16	5	F	24	5	F	12	5	T	10
6	T	4	6	T	7	6	F	23	6	F	11
7	F	14	7	F	10	7	T	21	7	T	14
8	T	15	8	T	15	8	F	8	8	T	9
9	F	18	9	F	20	9	T	14	9	T	21
10	T	5	10	T	23	10	F	11	10	T	13

TEST 5			TEST 6			TEST 7			TEST 8		
Q	A	R	Q	A	R	Q	A	R	Q	A	R
1	F	2	1	T	1	1	T	13	1	T	16
2	F	9	2	F	16	2	F	11	2	T	17
3	T	3	3	F	17d	3	T	3	3	T	12
4	T	4	4	T	15b	4	T	5	4	T	4
5	T	22	5	F	13	5	T	34	5	F	15
6	F	14	6	F	12	6	F	28	6	T	2
7	T	6	7	T	8	7	F	13	7	F	9
8	F	15	8	T	5	8	T	26	8	F	7
9	T	8	9	F	18d	9	F	33	9	T	18
10	T	10	10	T	15a	10	T	18	10	T	6

how well did you do?

0-1 wrong answers—excellent work

2-3 wrong answers—review errors carefully

4 or more wrong answers—restudy the lesson before going on to the next one

48

The FREENESS of Salvation

matthew 23:37

John 5:40

John 3:19

Proverbs 1:24

Acts 13:46

matthew 11 20

II Thessalonians 1:8

CPSIA information can be obtained at www.ICGtesting.com
Printed in the USA
LVOW10s0710020815

448514LV00001B/8/P